"All Gave Some
Some Gave All."

Sharon Bomhert
5-1-10

Author's books
Days That Should Have Been
At Dawn

At Dawn

The true story of PFC Alfred W. Beard

I CO 23RD REG 2ND INF DIV
NORMANDY

By: Sharon Lambert

iUniverse, Inc.
New York   Bloomington

At Dawn

Copyright © 2008 by Sharon Lambert

All rights reserved. No part of this book may be used or reproduced by any means, graphic, electronic, or mechanical, including photocopying, recording, taping or by any information storage retrieval system without the written permission of the publisher except in the case of brief quotations embodied in critical articles and reviews.

The views expressed in this work are solely those of the author and do not necessarily reflect the views of the publisher, and the publisher hereby disclaims any responsibility for them.
iUniverse books may be ordered through booksellers or by contacting:

iUniverse
1663 Liberty Drive
Bloomington, IN 47403
www.iuniverse.com
1-800-Authors (1-800-288-4677)

Because of the dynamic nature of the Internet, any Web addresses or links contained in this book may have changed since publication and may no longer be valid. The views expressed in this work are solely those of the author and do not necessarily reflect the views of the publisher, and the publisher hereby disclaims any responsibility for them.

ISBN: 978-0-595-53225-4 (pbk)
ISBN: 978-0-595-63287-9 (ebk)

Printed in the United States of America

DEDICATION

To my childhood friends in Rainbow Valley and the country fun we shared. To my new friends from far away places during World War II. To old friends listed in this book. To the loving memory of my wife Sybil whom I adored.

Alfred Beard

FOREWARD

From a carefree barefoot boy throwing rocks at copperhead snakes to entering WWII as a Combat Infantryman, Alfred Beard survives machine gun fire, snipers and bombardment from heavy artillery shelling in the 'Battle of St. Lo', France. His platoon, following orders to fix bayonets and move forward, met the deadliest snakes of all, SS troopers, Hitler's worst. Out of 360 men, 320 were killed or wounded. All in 48 hours time.

Alfred Beard's Battles and Campaigns were:
Normandy — Wounded
Rhineland Campaign
Northern France Campaign
Central Europe Campaign

Decorations and Citations
EAME Theatre Ribbon
Four Bronze Service Stars
WWII Victory Ribbon
American Theater Ribbon
Purple Heart
Good Conduct Medal

INTRODUCTION

I am now 85 years old and going downhill fast. Bill Ward tells me to put my war experiences down on paper so I will try. My memory seems to be getting a little dim now. I had a little talk with Jesus about it this morning. He said to tell it all and tell it true so I will give it my best.

Alfred Beard

Spring 2008

Heritage – The Beginning

My Great Grandfather, William Hendry, was born October 6, 1829 in Glasgow Scotland. As a young man he worked his passage on a sailing ship to America. In rough seas the ship was being rocked from side to side when the rope William was holding onto swung him far out over the water. As he swung back to the ship they had to pry his fingers from that rope.

William's wife was Elizabeth Clark and they made their home for a time in Illinois. The family had six children:

James	died in infancy		
Isabella	born in		1858
William Loyd	"	"	1860
John Clark	"	"	1862
Maggie J.	"	"	1866
George C.	"	"	1871

On April 13, 1864 William signed intent to become an U.S. Citizen at Washington County, Illinois. When traveling to Kansas a special pass had to be obtained to cross Missouri as the Civil War was being fought. William found the area southwest of Fredonia to his liking and purchased land by Rainbow Creek. The family traveled by covered wagon and team of oxen.

William was a big man over six feet tall. He drove a freight wagon to and from Humboldt, Kansas for supplies and farm equipment. Osage Indians camped just west of the homestead along Rainbow Creek and some of the supplies from Humboldt were to trade with the tribe.

On one return trip William's wife told him two of the Indians had been disrespectful to her. When the Osage gathered to trade, the two were pointed out and William promptly knocked their heads together and threw them over his fence. The on looking Osage laughed and said, "Two Man got'em, Two Man got'em." Fortunately the Osage thought the incident funny.

Their youngest daughter, Maggie, married Edgar William Beard, my Grandfather. To them were born; Roy William and Susie Ethel. Roy William married Mable Lilly Marlett, my parents.

William and Elizabeth were one of many Kansas pioneer families who traveled so far to make their home on a new frontier. William passed away on July 27, 1878 as he was nearing his 49th birthday.

To date six generations of the family have lived on the land they homesteaded.

William and Elizabeth Hendry

ORIGINAL.

STATE OF ILLINOIS, } ss. I, Wm Hendry
WASHINGTON, COUNTY. of Scotland

Do solemnly swear that it is my bonafide intention to become a Citizen of the United States, and to Renounce all allegiance and fidelity to any Prince, Potentate, State or Sovereign whatever, and particularly _____ Queen _____ of Gr. Brittain _____, of whom I am now a Subject. So help me GOD!

Subscribed and Sworn to before me, this 13 day of April, A. D. 1864. _____, Clerk.

William Hendry's "Intent to become a U.S. Citizen." Signed April 13, 1864 in Washington County, Illinois. It renounces all allegiance to the Queen of Great Britain.

Front side of special pass William Hendry had to sign to cross Missouri on his way to Kansas in 1861.

Pioneer of Kansas

This is to certify that

William Hendry

was a Kansas Pioneer who came to or was born in Kansas in _____ 1870 _____ and who settled in
_____ Wilson _____ county. This certificate is issued to honor those who have assisted in
making Kansas a Great State. This is issued to _____ Alfred W. Beard _____ ,
a direct descendant to the above named pioneer, who has proven the person named was indeed an Pioneer of Kansas.
The result of this being the preservation of the history of the State of Kansas.
Issued this _____ 6th _____ day of _____ November _____ 2000 _____

Patricia Michaelis
STATE ARCHIVIST

Lenore Kensett
PRESIDENT, KANSAS COUNCIL OF
GENEALOGICAL SOCIETIES

Acknowledgement of Pioneer Heritage.

PART I
Childhood

Alfred William Beard

CHAPTER 1

I was born February 25, 1923 on a cold snowy night with the help of a neighbor woman as midwife. The storm, I'm told, drifted the snow fencepost high. I was the second child born to Roy and Mable Beard; their first being a daughter, Margaret, born four years earlier.

Like most folks living in the country we farmed. In no time it seems I was six and had to go to school, which was a one-mile walk uphill south of our house at Greenridge. First grade didn't interest me much with all the sitting you had to do so when I had enough I would just run out the door and head for home. On one of these self-dismissals I found a big timber rattlesnake crossing the road. When he saw me he coiled and began hissing and blowing while raising his head up and down and swaying it from side to side. Along with the constant buzzing of his tail rattles he was putting on quite a show. I was too scared to pass him so I climbed the fence and ran a wide path thru the trees before coming out on the road again.

When I was old enough to help Dad I had the usual country boy chores; milking cows, feeding chickens and pigs, etc. Summers were spent running barefoot and learning to swim by wading out waist deep in the creek and dog paddling back to shore.

I was always poking around where I shouldn't be. This time it was on the backside of Moms' chicken house where I found the backbone of a large blacksnake with three glass eggs in a row. The glass eggs were used to get a hen to start setting if she hadn't already started on her own.

I earned my first nickel picking blackberries. Later on I collected bounty on crows at 5¢ each. I was in the money now and math became my favorite subject in school.

My folks didn't have a car, only horses and wagon for farm use. When we needed to go to Fredonia we walked to Grandpa's and he drove us. We also didn't have a radio so on some winter evenings we walked to Homer Stroud's house as he had one. About the coldest I ever remember getting was on the long walk over there during winter but it was all worth it to listen to that radio.

By 1931 or 1932 money was still scarce, so boys in Rainbow Valley would collect bounty on spring crows as I did after hunting and trapping all winter.

Sharon Lambert

In summer we could be waterboy at thrashing time, shock wheat and oats in the field at harvest time and drive horses on hay rakes or on the hay bucks at hay baling time. We could carry wood to the buzz saws in fall and winter and chop weeds in the fields when needed. This is a few ways we earned our spending money. I believe we were just as happy as folks are now.

My crowd consisted of the four Sissom boys; Eugene, Kenneth, Keith and later on Leland. There was also Glen Lambert, Oren Delaney and myself. I remember one hunting trip we all went on. Glen Lambert had the hunting dogs so we all got together and walked up to Oren Delaney's house which, at that time, was on the north side of a high hill just south of Fred Spellman's farm.

We had a few opossums we left at Oren's and all headed west around the big mound, then south into the next pasture where the dogs treed a civet cat. The civet was out on the limb of a hedge tree and we boys all gathered under the tree, except Oren. He said, "I'm going to stay way back because I have a date tomorrow and don't want any of that scent on me." We shot the civet and Oren was the only one that got any on him.

We then went west along the north side of the hill past where Dale Tharp now lives, on west to the creek and up to Pratt's pond and cattle pens. We hunted down the valley north of Pratt's cabin before finally heading back home. I was tired and sleepy by then but we had a bunch of opossums and skunks and one civet. When I finally got to bed it was around 3:00 A.M.

I also liked to fish along the Fall River. I rode my bicycle down to Tad Watkins place, which was east of Jerry McGinnis's farm. I went down to the river and set some limb lines. When I came out it was getting late. Tad came out of his little one room shack and said, "If you will just wait until dark my brother will be here and I want you to meet him." I told him I had some chores to do and needed to get home. When I got out on the road, that bicycle went faster than it ever had before or after. His brother had been dead for several years.

CHAPTER 2

There was a community meeting at Green Ridge School one evening. As me and the boys were walking up the hill from my house Lester Sissom drove past. He was in low gear so Glen and Oren jumped on his back bumper for a ride. Lester knew the boys were there so drove by the schoolhouse so fast they couldn't jump off. In fact, they couldn't get off until Lester was on the hill near the Buxton road. They had to walk back two miles. By the time we all got together the school was full of people and the program was under way. We tried watching thru a window but a big fat man sat there. Since it was the only window we could see thru Glen asked him nice if he would move but he just sat there. Glen went to Harvey Maxwell's pickup and got his electric stock prod. The fat guys seat was pressed against the window screen and Glen let him have it real good. That guy let out the biggest yell and nearly landed on the ones sitting next to him. We boys left for parts unknown as we had already seen our show.

At another school meeting, this time at Green Valley, there was a man from Fredonia that had his car wired so that if you touched it you would get a real strong electric shock. He liked to sit in the car and when you walked by he would start a conversation with you. If you put your hand on the car he would push a button and shock you. Glen knew this and said, "I'll fix that guy." He walked up close and put his hand on the window. When the man pressed the button Glen grabbed him by the ear, which pretty much ended his fun.

The young boys always went out on Halloween and pulled tricks on people. One night we all gathered in the valley and had Ray Kelsey and Lloyd Chisham in the group. We were in the process of taking all of one man's farm machinery a quarter of a mile down the road and putting it on a bridge into another man's gate. Before we got finished he heard us, came out of his house cussing like I had never heard before. We all hid in the road ditch for he was always shooting his shotgun. We found out later his wife took the gun away from him.

Another group was getting John Stover's equipment and doing the same thing only John ran out and hid in his wagon with his shotgun. When the boys were done and went to leave, John raised up and made them pull him back home.

Sharon Lambert

The Sissom boys and me were together from little guys on up to Army age. We were always on the creek fishing or swimming. We ran barefoot and none of us were ever bitten by a poisonous snake. There must have been guardian angels in Rainbow Valley. One day we were busy killing a big snake in the road on our way home from school. Rocks and clods were flying and a few clubs. A car drove up while the show was going on. A paper salesman got out and said, "What kind of snake did you just kill?" We told him we always called them chocolate drop snakes. He said, "You just killed a big copperhead." That was a surprise to us for we had killed a lot of them. We knew they were real sassy and full of fight but they were no match for a bunch of boys with clubs and rocks.

When I was in school, about the fourth grade, Warren Stover knocked on the door and told the teacher not to let us kids walk home alone for a mad dog had been seen in the area. She had the Penny kids, the Sissoms and my sister and me all stuffed in her car. We saw the dog laying in the hedgerow just over the hill. The men found and killed him the next day.

My Dad told about swimming as a boy at nearby Stroud's Ford. Fred Stroud could just lay on the water and float or he could be upright and tread water with his feet and look like he was standing on the bottom. One boy could not swim and asked Fred, "How deep is it?" Fred said, "This deep," pointing to his chest. The boy jumped in and they had to fish him out.

Not far from Stroud's I was swimming with a group of friends and a boy walked up and asked the same thing. We said it was deep enough to dive off the bank where he was standing. Now when we dove in we were hitting the water a few feet out. The boy dove in right next to the bank and stuck his head in the mud. He was more mad than hurt but learned a lesson.

Later on I was shocking wheat for Maxwell's and the bundles had been on the ground for a few days. I saw a snake that appeared to be asleep so I stomped his head with my heel. When I picked up my foot he struck my shoe and chased me for a few yards. When I saw he was a timber rattlesnake I threw my hat down by him and after he coiled up I found an old fence post and made snake hash. Ray Kelsey asked, "Did you have to kill him so dead?" He had four rattles.

Dad used to stack his wheat and oats then thrash the grain in the early fall. We killed eight copperheads out of five stacks one year. No telling how many got away in the weeds and grass around the stacks. Every man there wore rubber boots the next day.

Fred Smith came one day, said he wanted me to come after dinner to help saw wood. When I walked across the pasture going up to his place I saw a skunk go in a hole on a little mound of dirt. I stuck a stick of wood

At Dawn

in the hole to keep him in until I could come back. At Smith's I carried wood for about three hours and was paid a total of 35¢. On my way home I twisted eight skunks out of the hole and got $12.00 for them. Mom made me leave my clothes outside and take a bath. Oh well, I was rich now.

Homer and Mabel Stroud bought an 80-acre place southwest of Fall River, Kansas. I was helping them move up there from where they lived southwest of Fredonia. We had everything but his two big horses. I met Homer just south of New Albany, Kansas in the evening. He drove the car and I took my turn with the horses. I got to the oil field pump station southwest of New Albany about dark. I was riding one horse leading the other. When the pump station would pull the rods into pump, they would raise up about 18 inches in the air. We crossed over one rod but the next one raised in the air right in front of the horses scaring them. We ended up back down the road a ways. I got off and walked and led the horses back. When we got to the rod they pressed their heads into my back, leaned together and we went across the rod on the run. We were now on what they call The Wolftrail. I walked them awhile then would ride awhile. We got to Stroud's close to midnight. I was sure tired but I was young then. I stayed at Homer's until the cows and horses got settled down at their new home.

PART II
WAR

CHAPTER 3

When the U.S.A. entered the war I was working for Homer Stroud's neighbors near Fall River for $6.00 a week and my board. All my friends were being drafted into the Army. I tried to enlist but found out all farm hands were froze on the job. Jim Allen, Jr. told me he had signed up to go in the next bunch of draftees. I signed up also. They had called up three groups and not us so we went to the Draft Board and asked why. They said, "Go home and go to work. We're taking the pool hall boys first."

When they had thirteen of us they drafted one more and sent us to Leavenworth, Kansas on March 6th, 1943. We took our physical exam and came home for a week to tend to any business. We went back March 13th and were sworn into the Army for the duration of the war plus six months.

Jim Allen and I were separated. I went to Camp Campbell, Kentucky to train with an armored division. The tanks we were trained in were Sherman tanks with 9 cylinder airplane engines, which took high-octane gasoline. After seeing three of them catch fire and burn I was wanting a way out of them.

There were five crew members in a tank and we each had to do the other's job for one week. When it was my turn to drive we were in a convoy of five tanks and I was fourth in line. We were on land the Army had purchased from farmers and the farm buildings were still there. We had orders to put all hatches down, as in combat, and see through periscopes. There was so much dust I got off the road a little and suddenly there was a huge tree in front of me. I missed the tree but took out the corner of a barn.

Another day we formed a line from side to side and drove into trees that were so high we could barely see each other. My tank suddenly leaned so far it almost turned over so I turned and went downhill then back the original way. We were on the dam of a dry pond.

Next we were to travel on main roads. The tank had rubber tracks with steel cleats in them. We were going top speed of about 28 to 30 miles per hour on a concrete highway and had to make a right-hand turn. The tank slid sideways off the highway right against a railroad track and leaned over so far it scared me. I stopped but my tank commander was motioning for me to give it the gas so on we went.

15

Sharon Lambert

The following week I got to be the gunner. I shot some slabs painted white at 1000 yards, then I was on detail to put more slabs up for the next man. We were busy setting them upright when I heard some of the fanciest cussin' and yelling I ever heard. A dumb soldier was trying to drive a slab in the ground with an unfired high explosive shell.

On another training day an instructor was showing recruits how to use a gunners quadrant which was a small triangle with a level bubble on it. There was a chart that told the setting for so many yards out, then you would put it on the gun barrel, center the bubble and fire.

Now the instructor was reading a comic book instead of watching the recruit. The guy set the quadrant on the cannon barrel backwards, leveled the bubble and fired. The shell hit the ground a short way from the tank and exploded. There happened to be a high up officer in the area who got a piece of shrapnel through his pant leg. That night the officer was still out there with the instructor until about 11:00 o'clock. I think the comic books were thrown away after that.

Basic Training also taught us how to set off electric dynamite caps with flash light batteries. The instructor said, "All you do is put one wire on the ground and the other wire on the hot post." I told my buddy, "Duck, he's going to do it." It went off and the instructor had a cut arm and another a cut lip. The next day we had a new instructor.

Next we were being shown several different things. The first was a stick of dynamite with a wire like sand paper on it. The instructor said, "All you do is pull the string out and it will ignite the fuse." He handed it to a kid and said, "Here, hold this." He was going to show us the next thing on his list but the kid holding the dynamite tapped him on the arm and said, "Now what do I do with it?" He had already activated the fuse. The instructor grabbed it and threw it in a hole dug for that purpose, yelled "Fire in the hole," three times which was the warning to run, but the rest of us were already out and running. There were no dull moments in Basic Training.

At another session we were all sitting in a circle around our instructor when a man came walking by. He was wearing a uniform we weren't familiar with so we never paid much attention to him. At this same time we had a soldier in the group that had been on active duty in Africa and had been machine gunned across his middle. He had been so badly shot up that he was just with us until he could be discharged. He was sitting in our circle to pass the time away. Suddenly he started cussin' and tackled the man in the uniform. He got him down and was trying to choke him to death.

It turned out the man was wearing a German uniform just to see if we would recognize it. He was actually a German born in the states who could speak their language. They had not planned on a soldier out of combat

At Dawn

being among the new recruits. We never saw the man for a while as he had a pretty sore neck. After that deal we knew what a German uniform was.

An interesting thing happened in our chow line when a recruit, who was on the small side, saw his friend up ahead in the line. He walked up and got behind him. Now there was a tall smart mouth guy down the line who said, "Well, if he can do that, so can I." He went up and jerked the recruit out of line so hard he fell down. The next thing I saw was the little guy jumping about a foot and a half in the air and hitting the smart mouth on the chin three times, knocking him flat. He then picked up his mess kit and got back in line behind his friend. We found out he was the Bantamweight Champion from Bronx, New York.

The next time I saw this smart mouth he jumped a recruit who had his feet in the aisle. He pretended to trip, started an argument and slapped the young man across the face. The recruit stood up, put his hands on each side of the bully's head and said, "Now I don't want to hurt you." This really set the guy off. He drew his fist way back but before he could swing he was hit on the chin twice and knocked cold for half an hour.

He had the unfortunate luck to have picked on another professional boxer. This one was from Mississippi. When the slow learner woke up he said, "One of these days I'm going to find someone I can whip and I'm going to whip him everyday!" I just hope he made it to the front lines.

CHAPTER 4

After five months training they were sending us to other places. Some of us went to Ft. Benning, Georgia to go through paratroop training. I made it through the running and physical training but I have a fear of height so I was washed out. Now I was feeling real bad that I had failed and while I was waiting to be sent somewhere else I was handed a sawed off shotgun with three shells and three prisoners to guard. They told me that if one escaped I would take his place. The old Sarge in charge said if they tried anything to shoot them and have the others carry them in. One of them had killed his commanding officer and was in for life. One day he said, "I'm going to make you eat that gun," and came toward me. We were in a building with only one door and I stepped out in the hall and got ready to shoot, but when he came out he had cooled down.

They put him in solitary confinement and scolded me for not killing him. The prisoner yelled at me and said, "I know you're from Kansas and I'll hunt you up and kill you after the war."

While still at Ft. Benning, Georgia a soldier in my tent said, "If you will go with me to town tonight I'll show you some fun." So we went into Columbus, Georgia then went across the bridge over the Chattahoochee River into what they called Phenix City, Alabama, which I heard was the roughest town in the U.S.A.

Alabama was a wet state but Georgia was dry. We went into a bar then through swinging doors into a huge dance hall. It was about 3:00 o'clock in the afternoon and pretty near empty. By 4:00 o'clock people were coming in from everywhere. I had never seen a meaner looking group of people. I decided to leave but when I got to the swinging doors, two guys stepped in front of me and said, "No one leaves here until the show is over." They were not any bigger than me and civilians so I said O.K. and walked back a few steps, whirled around and hit them as fast as I could run at that distance. I got loose from them in the bar area. I got into the street, on across the bridge into Columbus and back to camp. The other soldier didn't come in until a few days later. The M.P.s and civilian cops raided the place and took them all to jail. When I look back on that escape I know God was giving me extra power to get out of there.

At Dawn

We were ordered out on a three-day bivouac on the Alabama side of Ft. Benning. I was guarding the cook tent one moonlit night when I saw what I thought was a big black dog coming towards me. When he got close I ran toward him stomping my feet. He turned and ran away woofin' somewhat like an old hog would. He ran right over a tent and just flattened it. A Lieutenant came crawling out and said, "Guard, what was that?"

"I think it was a black bear sir." I helped him set up his tent again and hoped he couldn't see me laughing.

We were sent to Camp Claiborne, Louisiana next to the 84th Infantry Division. They were taking in extra men to train for replacements for the D-Day landing but we didn't know about that yet. The day after I went to the 84th a little guy came in that I thought was a Mexican. He needed a shave so they had put him on K.P. He bunked next to me so I told him if he didn't shave he would be on K.P. the next day. He told me, "I no got money." I gave him $5.00 to get shaving material. He came back with the change but I told him to keep it until he got paid. His name was Ernest Pasada and for that kind deed I made one of the best friends I ever had. Later I asked him about why the whites didn't like him nor the Mexicans either. He said, "I am Spanish from California, not Mexican."

We had five Mexicans in our Company. One came in drunk one night and I heard an awful commotion at the other end of the barracks. I found out later that the Mexican had put a guy through a window. The next time, he came up to me and stuck a dagger under my nose as I was writing a letter. I shoved it aside and went on writing. He said, "You mean you no scared?" I said, "You know you're not going to hurt me." It was then my little Spanish friend jumped from an upper bunk with a dagger in his hand saying, "You leave him alone. He is my friend." They stood and glared at each other for a while then the Mexican threw back his head, laughed and left. Boy was I ever glad.

My Company was sent on a night patrol and I fell in an old open well. I managed to grab hold of some bushes and got out but it was a long way down to the water. Soon afterwards my 84th Division was sent on a long hike. The first day we walked 25 miles in a half circle. It rained on us the better part of the day. Our feet and shoes were wet and we were a very miserable bunch of guys. We slept on the ground that night then finished the circle the next day. Several fell out beside the road to be picked up by truck for the rest of the trip.

My buddy and me made it all the way but our feet were blistered and sore the next day. Only the ones who made it got a weekend pass so we went to town and sat in a bowling alley all the time so we wouldn't be put on guard duty or K.P.

Sharon Lambert

The hotel was so full we had to sleep on the floor in the hallway with a pillow and blanket but we didn't have to be on our feet for two days.

While we were still at Camp Claiborne we were sent out for three days of training but we camped at the same place each night. We had to dig a hole six feet deep and six feet wide on both sides for a garbage pit. When we were ready to leave the area we had two razorback pigs down in the pit. The Company Commander said, "Why don't you farm boys jump in and get the pigs out." We said, "We would rather not." A fella from New York City said, "You farmer boys make me sick." He then jumped in the pit to throw them out and there was never a better show at a rodeo or circus than the one we saw. He made it out alright but his pant legs were almost shredded to ribbons. The Commander said, "O.K. farm boys, how do we get them out?" We answered, "Just fill the hole up and leave one side clear so they can get away." This we did. You can imagine how mad those pigs were by the time they could get out but they took the open side to escape and everyone was happy except the guy with the torn up pant legs. He was a lot wiser now.

CHAPTER 5

I trained with the 84th Infantry until winter. I came home on furlough in February of 1944. When we got back to Camp Claiborne they called us all out and said, "We need volunteers for overseas duty." All of us single guys stepped forward. The Captain said, "I'm glad to see you do that. I was going to take you anyway."

We were put on a troop train the next day and went through New Orleans. We had a six-hour waiting period there on a sidetrack. Part of our train was coming from Texas with soldiers who had only five or six months of training. In any outfit, when they knew where you were from, they would never send more than one of you to the same Company. The reason was a close friend or relative getting killed was so much worse than a stranger to you. I did not have to be with a person over a few minutes to know whether I liked him or not.

It was getting dark when they pulled our car onto the main line ready to roll out. I told the Porter if there was anything he thought I should see to come and tell me. He came in later and said, "I think you should step out the end of the car and look around." It was night by now with a full moon. All I could see was water every direction. We were crossing the mouth of the Mississippi River, which was seven miles wide at that crossing. The Porter got a laugh out of me that time. Our engine was an old coal burner steam engine and part of the way the engineer was a heavy gray haired woman.

To me there is no sound any lonelier than a steam train or steamboat whistle. Our train went across Mississippi, Alabama, Georgia and headed north through the coastal states. In the Blue Ridge Mountains we went through a lot of tunnels. All of us suffered from the coal smoke from the engine. A few soldiers always had their windows open.

We were sent to Ft. Meade, Maryland first and went through more infiltration courses. Machine guns firing three feet over us and dynamite in post holes going off as we crawled by. During the same kind of courses at Fort Benning, a recruit was crawling along and looked up to see a rattlesnake in his path. He was able to reach out real quick and grab it. He carried it the rest of the way through the course. We saw a demo of our artillery that was timed to go off thirty feet above ground. The Germans didn't have that yet.

21

We were sent on to Camp Shanks, New York. Three feet of snow lay on the ground. I naturally was on K.P. and Richard Smith, a friend from grade school, came through the chow line. I never got to visit but a little with him there. The next day it was snowing again. We heard later they had 48 inches total.

Soon we had orders to march down to the coast and get on board a ship. In doing so we had to march past a barracks of WAC's. They stuck their heads out windows and sang, "We Don't Want Any Bacon, We Just Want A Piece Of The Rhine." We were put down below and went to bed about 11:30 p.m. We soon knew we were on our way by the vibration of the ship. When they let us up on deck the next morning we couldn't see land. They said we were 400 miles out. There must have been twenty or more Victory ships loaded with troops, two huge aircraft carriers and all kinds of battle ships among us for protection against German submarines. We traveled in a zigzag course to the coast of Spain then north to England. When a sub was spotted we had to go below deck. Once I saw planes going off the carrier like wasps off a nest before going down below. Three times we could hear depth charges going off. The sailors told us that every time there was oil surfaced so they must have got them.

We never lost a ship and were fourteen days going over. Our showers were sea water pumped from the ocean. They told us if we fell overboard we would last less than an hour. I only took one shower in fourteen days.

I could see some pretty houses along the coast of England. We were sent on to North Ireland for two weeks. One evening I was sitting on a big rock on the beach when a woman walked by and said, "I say me boy, ye might as well be merry for tomorrow ye may be dead." I didn't even answer her. In a little while a soldier came walking by and it was Richard Smith again. When we were sent from North Ireland to England the boat was so overloaded we slept up on deck side by side. Richard and I talked all night. We were separated in England but I found him on the battlefield in France later. No one knew yet but D-Day was soon to come.

A soldier in the 2nd Infantry Division broke a leg on maneuvers in England so I was put in his place in K Company, 23rd Regiment. Just before D-Day I got the mumps and was sent to Wales for twenty-one days. Afterwards I was sent across the Channel and landed at Omaha Beach, France. The Military had gained fourteen miles inland in twenty-one days. I was with a little short soldier from the 2nd Division and he kept telling me, "You won't have a chance. We've had four years training and you only had eleven months." It did worry me some. We got on a truck that took us to five miles from the front lines. The driver wouldn't go any closer so we walked on in. When we got there I heard some guns going off a few miles away. A soldier raised up in a foxhole and said, "You better find you a hole because they're on the way." Me and my little buddy saw an empty foxhole and ran for it. Just as we jumped in the shells started landing all around us. My little buddy went to pieces and started crying. So much for his four years of training. They took him out the next day.

The Commander came to me after the artillery quit. He said, "If you want to ask me anything just walk up and say, 'Hey Buddy,' but do NOT salute me. I want to live just as much as you do." Officers were always a target for snipers.

I had been sent to I Company this time so I asked why. They said I would have been a stranger to my Company anyway. That was something to think about. I was learning fast. We were just holding ground for eight days waiting for more replacements and equipment for another battle. I went on night patrol behind German lines. Was I scared? Yeees!

We were lucky and all came back. Next I was sent on outpost. This is being sent out half way between our lines and theirs trying to see all you can see and not be seen. We saw thirteen Germans carrying ammo to a gun emplacement but couldn't locate where until they fired it. They had a sniper in an old barn who must have seen one of us for they fired a 20 mm machine gun all around our location.

There were five U.S. fighter planes that bombed an antiaircraft gun about two miles from us but two planes were shot down. One came over our lines but the other was turned around and went over German lines. We couldn't help him.

We tried to sleep in the daytime but there was very little sleeping or eating for between the lines were the dead from both sides. There are no words to describe the awful odor. They started shelling one evening and eight of us dove in a foxhole that was covered with dirt and logs. One shell hit the dirt pile but we were only scared. The good Lord was certainly with us.

Our front line was a 30 caliber machine gun placed about thirty or forty yards apart with us Infantry boys in foxholes in between them. One night a German patrol came from behind us and just a little way from me. Three were shot and the rest got away.

The Germans used cat calls at night to verify positions. One night they sounded close by so I tossed out a grenade. The next morning we found a dead black cat that had run out of luck.

CHAPTER 6

At times we slept in our gas masks for the threat of poison gas was very real. We were told it would smell like new mown hay. On the night of the eighth day we were told to leave our positions at the first gray sky at dawn, withdraw 400 yards and get in foxholes. This was to be the worst and longest day of my life.

First the bombers came, both the American and English. They were flying over us continually for 1 ½ to 2 hours. Then our artillery started firing over us but so did the German artillery. This lasted until about 9:00 o'clock in the morning. There was a lull and we were told to attach bayonets and go. A soldier dropped his bayonet so I handed it to him. He was so shell shocked and numb he dropped it again. I handed it to another and said, "Here, he don't want it."

Before we had reached our original front lines the Germans started shelling again. They were starting to retreat and were slowing us down. Our only protection was to lay as flat as we could.

Shells were exploding in every direction. One hit so close the concussion rolled me over. The shells would bury in the soft ground and the shrapnel would go up and out at an angle. My head was against my buddy's boots. I yelled, "Come on, let's go." He didn't move. He had raised up to look and a piece of shrapnel had hit him in the forehead. That was the first one so close to me and it made me real sick.

I got a chance to run forward again and found some more of my buddies. We all started again but the shelling did too. I hid between a cannon tire and sand bags. On the next move we got in a German foxhole. Eight of us in a two-man hole. There was a soldier in the hole that had been shot in the shoulder who came from my schoolmate, Richard Smith's, platoon. He said Richard was killed. His platoon had gone ahead of us and the Germans had let them pass, then machine-gunned them from both sides of the hilltop.

When we went down the valley I found Richard. (After all these years I still can't tell it without breaking down.) By this time we had only gone about one mile. The main German army had already pulled back. We had to run down a hedgerow then turn to the left and clean a forest out. While we were running a sniper killed the man in front of me. We got the sniper

At Dawn

and came to an open field. This was near St. Lo in France. The Germans were in tanks behind hedgerows out of sight. They let us all get out in the field and then started shelling us with everything they had. Soldiers were being killed everywhere you looked. I was watching one soldier running toward me when there was a blinding flash of fire, then nothing. He was just blown away.

Those of us who crossed this field of death came to the timber. Two of us went past big trees that had been bombed down. Laying over a tree on his side was a dead SS officer. His pistol and holster was sticking up just tempting you to reach out and take it. I told my buddy we better leave it for no doubt it was booby-trapped and I wanted to go home at war's end.

The Germans had left some Polish prisoners, young kids and old men behind to slow us down. They would fire a burst of machine gun fire over us and as we hit the dirt they would come out with hands up. My platoon had 21 prisoners when we ran into some SS troopers, Hitler's worst. They pinned us down with machine gun fire then called in artillery on us. We got the machine gunner and a fighter plane bombed the tank that was shelling us. I believe they carried a 250 lb. bomb. The explosion picked me up from the foxhole I was in and turned me upside down and stuck my face in the dirt. How God saved me from all that had been happening I'll never know. I was so tired I didn't think I could keep up but just then a big shell came crashing through the brush and on past me that hadn't exploded yet. It scared me so bad I started running, caught up with my platoon and passed them.

We were soon stopped by another SS trooper with a machine gun. I was behind a big tree when a shell came screaming in. You could always tell when they were going to be very close by their sound. Suddenly I heard a voice say, "Get away from that tree." I took three running steps and dove to the ground just as the shell hit a limb over where I had been. Two pieces of shrapnel hit me in the right leg. One the size of a pea stuck in the bone. The other the size of my thumbnail cracked the bone near the knee. There was so much pain for a few seconds I could hardly stand it. Shrapnel hits red-hot. My leg then went numb and stayed that way until I reached England 5 days later.

The ground was torn up like a garden spot where I had been laying. It was then that I realized there was no one there to tell me to move. It had to be the good Lord. This was about 3:00 or 4:00 o'clock in the afternoon. I found out later our Company Commander and our Medics were killed. Soon another piece of shrapnel hit me in the ribs hard enough to bruise me. It was still very hot but I put it in my pocket for a souvenir.

25

I was put in a foxhole with a soldier that had his arm and back riddled with shrapnel and was out of his head. I was to try to keep him quiet but he begged for water all night but there was none to be had. The next morning I was put in a captured German command post. A twelve-foot hole each way and about six foot deep covered with logs and dirt. They gave my rifle and bayonet to another soldier and gave me a carbine and a wounded SS trooper to guard. I was in one corner and he in the other. I was told if he moved to shoot so we sat and glared at each other for almost three hours. Then three soldiers came with water and ammo and took me back with them. It was then a call came on the radio asking how many men there were to carry on. He said, "Forty Sir." Out of 360 men, 320 were killed or wounded. All in 48 hours time. The worst was over for me but there still was a lot of work for the Lord to bring me home. What I went through in those 48 hours I cannot forget in a lifetime.

When the three soldiers took me out with them I used my good leg and had my arms around their necks. I was so thirsty I could have spit dust but I wouldn't use the water that was brought in. We came across a dead American soldier from the battle the day before. I checked his canteen, which was half full and drank the water. Those guys gave me some strange looks but I told them, "He isn't going to drink it." You get a little dingy on the battlefield.

We came upon a German soldier sitting on a stream bank just like he was resting. I told them he was killed by concussion, which froze you in whatever position you were in. They wouldn't believe me until I shoved him over.

We came to the hedgerow we ran down the day before. It had a row of circles of white tape all along it. Someone with a mine detector had marked the antitank mines which we had run through the day before and were not heavy enough to set off. We came to a blacktop road where I was put on a jeep for the rest of the way.

We were going up a little hill and around a curve when the driver said, "Hold on, this curve is hot." We skidded around the curve and a shell exploded behind us. He took me on to a First Aid station. Every place I went they tried to give me a morphine shot but I told them to save it for someone else that my leg was still numb.

As soon as we had enough soldiers to fill the ambulance he took us to Omaha Beach to a big hospital tent. I saw my first Army nurse there. The nurses were the same as angels to me. A Red Cross woman came by and wrote out a list of what we needed. To give you an idea of what we looked like, we had about a thirty-day growth of whiskers with soot off of the cans of coffee that was brought to us from behind the lines. That was to conceal our faces when the Germans fired up flares at night. I was given a shave that evening and the next day the Red Cross woman didn't know me when she brought my things.

I asked the nurse what we were to do if we were bombed in the night. She said, "Don't worry, there is a big white cross on top of the tent. They won't bomb us." I asked why she wore a steel helmet and what were the jagged holes in the tent wall from? She said, "Oh shut up." That night the German planes flew over low and dropped their bombs close to us. We all were laying on the ground the next morning.

The following day a C-47 Flying Boxcar landed on the beach on a steel mat runway, just two narrow strips on the sand. They loaded twelve of us on stretchers strapped to the inside of the plane. The pilot asked us to leave our shoes and steel helmets behind or he would be overloaded. I said, "I'll leave my pants if that would help!"

We went way up at first to find smooth air but so many complained about their ears hurting that he came down to twenty feet above the waves. Now I was on the wall higher than the pilot so it looked to me like we were going to hit every wave.

When we got to the English coast we had to go high again and circle until we could land at the London airport. After landing we were put on a hospital train to go to the 94th General Hospital at South Hampton. This was five days from the time I was wounded and my leg remained numb. Thank you again Lord.

I had not eaten anything all this time. They were so busy at the hospital they could not take time to look for the steel in my leg so they reamed out the jagged holes, packed gauze covered with salve in the holes then put a cast on top of everything. When I came out from whatever they put me out with, a nurse brought me a bowl of soup made from dehydrated peas, which was not my favorite food. The soldier in the next bed said when I had eaten the soup I told the nurse I wanted to shake the Mess Sergeant's hand for that was the best meal I ever ate.

I was reminded of the time we were just holding ground on the front lines in Normandy while waiting for more replacements to come in. There was an extra big artillery shell came in one day and blew a hole about three feet deep and four feet across the top. Now there was an old saying that shells never hit the same place twice. We were eating rations that had cans of cheese in them that we called plastic cheese for I don't think it was possible to digest it. We threw the cans in the shell hole and covered them up. In a few days another shell hit in the exact same place and blew ribbons and strings of cheese all over the trees and weeds around that hole. We were threatened that we weren't going to get any more rations for a

Sharon Lambert

while if we didn't eat our cheese. That never bothered us much for we were always hungry anyway.

We broke through the German lines the day I was wounded. We were part of the 1st Army. General Patton was over the 3rd Army. Patton made news when he lined up a lot of tanks, four abreast, to drive into Paris, France but had gotten ahead of his supply line and ran out of gas before entering the city. That was the news when I got to the hospital in England.

My mail finally caught up with me while at the hospital. In it was a letter from Richard Smith whom I had just recently seen laying dead on the battlefield near St. Lo. He was saying how much he was looking forward to us going home soon. It was a hard day.

CHAPTER 7

The hospital was full of the wounded and each of us was thankful to be there. All had to deal with flashbacks of war; the things we saw, the sounds of heavy artillery and 'Screaming Meemies' which was an attachment on German artillery shells mainly to scare us. It did work on the nerves. Germans called our 155 mm cannon 'The Whispering Death' because of its sound.

I learned to walk on those crutches pretty good. When the cast was removed there was gauze sticking up from the holes in my leg. The Doc missed his grab for the first piece but got it on the second try. They almost had to set on me for the other one. Until they healed up they were still mighty sore when I walked.

We moved into tents for awhile and took short marches to get back in shape. Another soldier and I would go to the sawdust pit they had for training and practice throwing each other over our heads. It soon paid off for I ran into a Corporal that was a bully. He walked by as I was sitting on my bed and made a smart crack about my leg being in his way. I made a smart crack right back and he whirled around and said, "Why you." He lunged at me and grabbed me by the neck. He was mad and hurting me so I caught both elbows, put my good leg in his middle and overhead he went. I turned loose as he went over and he lit on his side across the next bedrail, got up and left holding his side. He never bothered me again.

We were camped in tents near a British airfield and were being bombed nearly every night. We had to take shelter in an open trench that had about a foot of water in it. We all had to duck down and cover our heads as best we could until the bombing ceased. We were given sleeping bags with wool liners that had zippers. We were afraid to use the liners because we never knew when we would have to make a fast dash for the air raid trench. I used my liner for a pillow. The man next to me said, "Well I'm going to use my liner," and proceeded to cut the bottom open. When bombs dropped close he just pulled up the liner around his knees and ran for cover. He usually beat the rest of us.

The Australians and Canadians were O.K. and treated the Americans well. Some British didn't and we had conflict on several occasions. I was walking with Robert Walker from Lake Charles, Louisiana and

Sharon Lambert

two Canadian WAC's. We met two British Air Force officers and they popped off some things they shouldn't have. We went a short way when Robert said, "I'll be right back. I want to speak to those two." I heard a thump, thump and turned to see both British on the ground. Now I was remembering the boxers from a previous camp and asked, "How long were you in the ring?"

"Nine years." he said. The professional boxers I knew were all respectful and very polite, never looking for a fight. That's why I liked them.

The next day a tall soldier from Alabama said, "Let's have some fun." The Queen of England was supposed to visit the hospital that day so a group of nurses were in their dress uniforms and lined up near the road. I never saw so many angels in one group before, next were the M.P.s in their dress uniforms. We all stayed in between the buildings a long way back. Now Alabama sure wasn't in the hospital for his legs for he could run like a rodeo clown. The hospital buildings were surrounded by timber so Alabama went to the back of the nurses and started singing, "Oh she'll be coming around the mountain when she comes." The M.P.s took after him and the nurses were all laughing. The M.P.s didn't find him and came back and got in formation when Alabama started again in the opposite direction, "Oh she'll be wearing red pajamas when she comes." The race was on again.

When it was time for dinner we formed a line in front of the Mess Hall. Some of the M.P.s tried to make us leave but a General came along and told them to leave us alone. He said, "There's not a man here that wouldn't rather see his Grandmother than the Queen of England." Alabama showed up in time to eat and I don't believe the Queen ever did come.

Two of us went into town one night and forgot about England being blacked out. We got lost and had to get the M.P.s to take us to the pick-up spot.

On another outing into town I was with a former paratrooper who was recovering from a broken leg. We were going back to camp the back way and down an alley so we wouldn't have to show a pass to the guard. We hadn't gone far down that alley when we saw that some southern boys had blocked off the alley up ahead and behind us. I thought things were getting a little stressful when my friend pulled out his 45 semi-automatic pistol and worked the action to load. When we looked up the alley was clear. He said, "Remind me to get some shells for this thing."

We had a small guy in our group that came in drunk one night and was snoring loud. His name was Birdsong from Missouri. Four of us slowly lifted his bed, eased him down the steps and left him outside all night. He didn't wake up until the next morning. We tried it again later on

At Dawn

but he woke up as we were going down the steps and started swinging at the man closest to him. We dropped him, bed and all, and ran back inside. He stormed in but found that everybody was 'sound asleep.'

At one time we were at a place in England called Litchfield. Walt Reinhart was a truck driver there but I never met him. I surely was in his truck sometime while there. They were real strict in that camp so I didn't try anything out of the rules. Every evening they would announce over the loud speaker that Private or whatever rank he held, give his name - then announce like, 'Private Joe Blow gets 40 days in the guardhouse and fined $40.00.' Those of us that were a little timid never tried anything.

By now the Germans were sending their rocket bombs and robot plane bombs to England and all the port towns of France and Belgium and on into Holland. I believe the V-2 rocket was fired 70 miles into the sky, went into an arc and landed in England, mostly London. They were working on one to send to the United States but thank God we never gave them enough time to perfect it.

The robot plane bomb was not as large but there were so many more of them. They were like a small plane with a ram jet engine on top that sounded like a Model T Ford on two cylinders. They were sent on a given course and when they ran out of fuel they would crash. Some would glide straight ahead about ¼ mile, others would veer off to either side and some would come straight down. This would certainly work on your nerves at night. The British Air Force patrolled the English Channel to shoot them down. That got boring for some so they would fly along beside the bomb, put their wing tip on its wing tip and head it into the ocean.

We were nearing the time to cross the English Channel again. The first time the sea was so calm we went over the side of the ship on a cargo net and dropped into a landing barge to go ashore. This time the sea was so rough we had to throw our barrack bags into a large canvas chute held by two sailors. We had to jump in next and go down like a slipper slide, then grab your bag and get out of the way of the next man. It was about 35 feet down to the flat bottom landing boat. I saw two big sailors, one on each side of the chute, and wondered why they were there. We soon found out for a Company of southern guys followed us and some wouldn't jump in so those big sailors would throw them in headfirst. When they came down you could hear a 35-foot scream. We had stayed on the ship overnight for the sea was too rough to unload.

It was Thanksgiving Day so they fed our Thanksgiving dinner to the French kids at LeHavre. We were glad for the town of LeHavre was a pile of bombed buildings, which had been bombed to get the Germans out.

Sharon Lambert

My company landed just before dark at the edge of LeHavre. The ground was wet but they had squad tents set up with straw on the ground to lay on. A squad tent held eight men. There were two of us that needed a bathroom very bad. We saw a cow shed nearby with a wood gate in front so over we went. The next morning there was a very hot Sergeant yelling something about, "If I find out who went to the bathroom in the storeroom I will personally give them a good whipping." Two of us were very quiet. We were told in Basic Training that it's not what you did in this man's Army that counted, it's what you got away with."

When our troops ran the Germans out of a town, the free French would come out of hiding places and collect all of the French women that had lived with the German soldiers, shave their heads, strip their clothing off and run them through town throwing rocks at them. Almost like Bible times.

CHAPTER 8

We first went to a camp that had mud everywhere. Almost as bad as a cattle pen in a feed lot. I had wet feet for two weeks. While on K.P. one day the cook gave me a bucket of lard and tallow. I was to take it to the trash burner, melt it down and burn it. By the time I melted it my shoes were getting dry so I held them in the melted grease. I had dry feet for a few days.

We lived in a building that had the windows all broken out by bombs or artillery shells. There was a coal stove but no stovepipe so we hunted up some pipe and built a big fire. Our pipe turned out to be sink drain pipe and melted down. So much for that project.

We were put on a train that was in World War I. The cars were called 40 & 8. They were to haul 40 soldiers or 8 horses during that war. We men were loaded up so many in a car we had sitting room only. It took us several days to travel to Liege, Belgium at about 10 or 15 miles an hour. We were put off on a sidetrack when a French passenger train went by. When their train stopped, two of us climbed onto some open top cars and handed two cases of something down to the guys and hid them in our car. When we started out again a Lieutenant jumped to the ground up ahead of us and when we came past him he jumped up in our car. We supposed we were in trouble but he said, "Bring it out and see what we got." Both had big cans of fruit cocktail in them so we all had a real treat.

It was December and after being in Liege, Belgium for awhile, nineteen of us were put on a truck to Maastricht, Holland to be guards for a group of mostly welders and machinists that had just come over. They had welders and lathes to fix about anything that broke in the war. They even had a carpenter. We arrived about midnight and knew something big was going on for the flashes of many cannons lit the sky about six miles from our road into Maastricht. That turned out to be the spearhead of the "Battle of the Bulge." The Germans' plan was to go all the way to the coast and if they had, we would have been in bad trouble. This "Battle of the Bulge" was their last big try to stop us from going any further.

The night we arrived in Maastricht the cook stayed up and warmed a big dishpan of fish cakes he had prepared as it was a Friday but the new guys wouldn't eat them. The nineteen of us ate them all, even the crumbs.

Sharon Lambert

The cook had tears in his eyes and said, "At last I've found someone who likes my cooking." In the days following, when going through his chow line, he would give us extra servings but told the welders and repairmen to, "Move on." Oh, we were in good with that cook.

The morning after we arrived we were called out on the west side of our building by the Co. Commander and 1st Sergeant for roll call and to get our orders. Before we got started, a German plane came in low with machine guns chattering. I think he was after our vehicles. Nineteen guys went into the basement through an open window in about ten seconds. When we came back the Co. Commander and 1st Sergeant were just standing facing each other saying, "You know, we could have been killed." All that saved them was an eight-foot wall around the building. They said, "You soldiers sure know how to take care of yourselves."

On New Years Eve 1944 another German plane flew over low and someone threw open a window of our barracks. The pilot circled and came back over dropping antipersonnel bombs in a cluster. They would then break apart and spread out. Each small hand grenade size bomb had fins. They blew five holes over our heads in the roof, flattened all the tires on our trucks but only wounded one man when a bomb hit on the windowsill and shrapnel got him in the arm.

The next morning we were all called out in formation, the guards out in front. The Co. Commander told us guards that if anyone ever opened a window again to shoot out the lights. The windows were all painted black and we never had any more trouble. We had a little buck Sergeant with us and the Co. Commander said, "You will have to take orders from no one but him and me. I will give him orders every morning and he will give them to you."

There were about six big search lights in Maastricht, Holland searching the sky for enemy planes all night. If a plane dropped bombs, our orders were to run to the basement then back on guard as soon as the bomb went off. One night I was on duty on the south side of our building when the spotlight had a German plane really lit up. Antiaircraft was getting close to him. He was straight overhead and went into a dive. I went for the basement as fast as I could run. When I hit the door in, our 1st Sergeant was running out. He went "Ooofff." I got loose and on down to the basement. The plane came out of his dive and escaped and I went back on guard. As I was walking the other side of the building a snowball hit me beside the head. A young lady threw it from a balcony. I threw one back but she ducked and it broke a window. I apologized and told her I would pay for it the next day but she just laughed and said, "Never mind, it was my fault." Funny things can happen in war.

At Dawn

Our head cook had an uncle that lived in Maastricht. Four of us would give him our allotted packs of cigarettes and he would trade them for onions and bacon to season our powdered eggs with.

Just before we headed into Germany some of us went to the far side of town. The river we crossed was the Meuse River. The bridge was over a quarter of a mile across. I had crossed over in the afternoon and was right in the middle going back when I heard a loud roaring. I looked downstream and saw a German plane coming right above the water. I first thought he was going to bomb the bridge. Was I ever scared. It was too far to run, too high to jump so I just laid down and prayed. As it turned out, two P-38 planes were after him. He was more scared than I was. I got to look at the bottom of his plane only a few feet away as he went up over the bridge. Is it any wonder I still have nightmares?

We entered into Germany and the Germans were on the run so we knew it was just a matter of time until the wars end. I was always in the advance party when we moved ahead for some reason. We usually had both of our Lieutenants with us. Guard duty could be, on 4 off 4, or on 4 off 8, on 4 off 12 or 16 hours depending on how they spread us out. I sure got sleepy when we were on 4 and off 4 because they wouldn't be quiet so we could sleep.

One of our Lieutenants was a swell guy, the other was not. One real dark night I was guarding the main gate into our area. I, not being so brave, was sitting in a dark place so anyone who walked up would be where I could see his top half against the sky. I heard gravel crunching and here came the Lieutenant who was not so good. Instead of challenging like the book rules said, I just slipped in behind him as he took hold of the gate and rattled it saying, "GUARD." I stuck my gun in his back and said, "HERE." He almost went over the gate and he never checked a guard again. Our guns were loaded by then.

When we were in the Argonne Forest we moved ahead, set up a place for the Company and had plenty of spare time. Obie Ligon from Kentucky and myself slipped out and shot two deer with our carbines, took them to camp and dressed them out. Now Mr. Good Lieutenant had to argue with Mr. Not-So-Good so we could eat them instead of just throwing them away. Later our supply Sergeant slipped around and gave us the shells we had shot because Mr. Bad Lieutenant had an inspection set for us. I doubt he ever figured that one out. Anyway, he ate more than anyone else.

We went to the M.P.s who collected the guns from civilians. I picked out two 8 mm rifles. We could find machine gun belts full of ammo laying everywhere. Later I sent the guns home.

One evening things were a little dull so I built a fire in an air raid shelter, put on two machine gun belts of live rounds and got back to my post. I never heard fire crackers sound off any better. I emptied the building of guys for a little while. Pretty soon Mr. Good Lieutenant walked out where I was, stood and talked awhile then said, "It seems strange to me that the only person that should have been excited ... wasn't." I was glad he was the one who came out.

We tried dropping German hand grenades into a canal to get some fish but the water was too swift.

In France, Belgium and Holland we never walked in paths for the Germans left "Bouncing Betty" mines behind. All you could see were wires sticking up like a small TV antenna. If you bumped into them it would set off a small charge and a thing about the size of a Ford oil filter would bounce up about three feet in the air then would explode sending steel balls in every direction. The only way to live through one was to stand on it and lose your foot.

The Germans left behind all kinds of antitank mines, which a man on foot wasn't heavy enough to set off. We found lots of small mounds that were little concrete rooms covered with dirt. What they were used for we could only imagine. The door on one was cracked slightly open. I looked over the top and as my eyes adjusted to the gloom, I saw a 240 mm artillery shell in one corner with attached wiring running along the wall over to the door. That's all I needed to see. We left them to the detonation crews to destroy.

We moved into a town close to the Rhine River which had a big concentration of railroad tracks going through. The Allied Army left a pocket of Germans on the other side of the Rhine that were in caves in the mountains so they just by-passed them. The Germans had a rocket launcher on rails that they would pull out every night and fire three rockets at our town trying to destroy the railroad. They would then shove the rocket launcher back in the cave.

Now we had a welder that was very hard of hearing who slept on the upstairs floor by himself. We tried to tell him about the rockets but he wouldn't listen to us. One day our heavy artillery moved in five 240-millimeter cannons, set them up just behind our building. They fired one round at the cave to get the range set up and waited. Mr. Hard-of-Hearing moved to the basement immediately and we couldn't explain to him that it was our gun.

That night Germans fired one rocket and our big guns fired several rounds. No more rockets ever came. All the windows were broken out of the west side of our building and we couldn't talk that welder out of the basement. *

*(Soldiers that had been wounded and were able to return to Normandy were put under limited service. Usually no closer than two miles from the front lines. They were frequently bombed and strafed by planes as well as targeted by heavy artillery. Many served as guards enabling the others to do their job. They remained a vital part of the war effort having a part in every campaign.)

CHAPTER 9

The front lines were moving fast now. We soon crossed the Rhine River on a pontoon bridge General Patton had built out of German coal barges. We saw an entire German train that was crossing the valley when our planes bombed the bridge. That was a huge pile of junk.

At another location we had a truckload of supplies arrive just as a robot bomb came in. We all headed down in an air raid shelter but the driver took off running across a field. Later our Commander asked him why he did that instead of coming inside the shelter. He said, "Sir, I feel so much better if I can do something about it."

Another Company had a trucker taking soldiers to the front lines when a plane flew over and strafed them. The driver jumped out and ran, letting the truck go into a ditch. It tipped over on its side with a full load of men who had to walk on to the front lines on foot.

We were on the move so much it's hard to remember now just what all we did. We were in a town named Kirchheim, Germany and about dark the antiaircraft were firing all around us but we couldn't see any planes. We learned the next morning that Germany had surrendered. It was time to praise God.

We loaded up everything and headed out. I can't remember much about the trip out for I wasn't scared then. When we went through the Siegfried Line of huge concrete pill boxes, one was standing on edge where a bomb had hit right beside it. The dead were still inside for we smelled that horrible stink that can only come from human flesh. We ended up on a mountain top five miles from Liege, Belgium again. We stayed there two weeks. I went into Liege and Wally White and Wendel Cunningham were still there. I still had to pull guard duty at the gate. On some free time a friend and I went to a pub where they were playing the most beautiful music. Now I don't drink but you had to order if you wanted to sit at a table. We ordered two beers and he drank his down a little and I passed him my glass and he gave me his. He slowly drank it down some and passed it back to me. We did this until he had finished both our drinks. I certainly enjoyed the music that day.

While I was in Liege I walked across town to explore some of the city I had not seen before. I remembered I had crossed a bridge over a canal and was on my way back to our living quarters. It was getting late, soon to be dark, and we were still in black out rules. As I entered the bridge an Army nurse was standing there who was a 1st Lieutenant. She said, "Soldier, I want you to walk me to the hospital." I said, "Yes Ma'am." I walked her to the hospital but it put me late getting back but I knew the way even in the dark. I believe she had seen a man in the shadows over that bridge and needed an escort. I saw him too as he was slipping away.

She invited me to dinner the next day as a thank you. After taking her to the hospital I had to get back and was running fast until I realized another soldier was running as fast as he could go ahead of me. He thought I was after him so I turned and ran a block to the left and continued on my way to camp. I knew if I didn't that a fair size party of those southern boys could be waiting for me up ahead.

The following day I met the nurse for dinner and she said, "If anyone questions us I will handle it." Enlisted men weren't supposed to socialize with officers. At dinner we were challenged all right. A Major walked up and said, "What is this?" She said, "He is my brother." After that we were left alone. Her name was Zeda Pitcock from Oregon. When we finished eating I said, "Well Sis, I'll be moving out soon and might not get to see you again." And I never did.

While in Liege there was a Company of southern boys stationed near us. There were seven in the group causing a lot of trouble by taking over a bar in the town. They had sewn razor blades in their hats and when one of our group entered the bar they would slash his face.

An M.P. came to us guards and said he needed volunteers to help round them up. The M.P. had a truck back up to the front while nineteen of us armed guards entered from the back. When those boys saw us we didn't have to say a thing, they just marched out the front door. The M.P. was standing there with a 45 pistol in his hand and pointed to the back of the truck. That's all he had to do. They loaded up and were taken away.

On guard duty another night I heard a sound like; clack clack clack coming down the street. It was a young woman wearing wooden soled shoes who was being chased by a man. I shouted, "Halt" three times, which he ignored, then I fired. He turned and ran in between two buildings that were so close together no one could have gotten through, but he did.

One night a soldier came running up to me saying he wanted me to go with him. He said, "There is a ghost of a German soldier standing by the road." I told him I could not leave my post but I would go with him the next day. When we arrived at the place where he had seen the ghost, I saw a cross with a German helmet on it that was out in a field, so what he saw standing by the road I'm not going to say.

Sharon Lambert

We loaded up in trucks and went to LeHavre again. Now that the war had ended carnivals sprang up all along the French coast. One evening I walked to one. Just as I entered the area a young French girl slid her arm in mine and pointed at a Ferris wheel. She couldn't speak English and I couldn't speak French. We rode everything they had then she spun me around, pulled my head down and planted a big kiss on my mouth, turned and ran into the crowd. I walked back to my tent about eight inches in the air.

There was a woman wrestler in the carnival that would take on anyone. We had a guy who thought he was good so he said, "I'm going to make a monkey out of her." The next day his arm was in a sling and he could hardly walk. I wondered who the monkey was.

We stayed there two weeks, loaded up and returned to Belgium. I realized all this was to keep us out of trouble for they were shipping soldiers home as fast as they could find boats to carry us.

I was sent to Brussels, Belgium along with a lot of others for three weeks of rest camp. That was all of the treatment I got for combat fatigue, followed by a shot of insulin at 6:00 o'clock in the morning and we ate at 9:00 o'clock. That was to gain back our weight loss, which was down from 160 to 135 pounds for me.

All the American soldiers could ride the streetcars free. It was on one of them that I was pick pocketed and lost my address book. I had my wallet in another pocket and kept it. I've missed that address book ever since as it held the addresses of all my friends and buddies met during the war.

I was walking along the shops in Brussels and saw a nice sweater in the window that I wanted for my sister. I went in and the saleslady didn't speak English but communicated that the sweater was only a display item, that she didn't have any for sale as they were 'kaputt.'

There was nearly a civil uprising while we were there. King Leopold III had handed over Belgium to the Nazi's, which caused a lot of hatred. People would come out at night and write 'Abdication' on walls and streets and 'King Leopold equals Nazism.'

We were all sent back to the beach in LeHavre where we were the first time. I had been over about a year when I asked a soldier, "How long do you have to be here to get over being homesick?" He said, "Eighteen months." He was right. I was over there twenty-two months and after eighteen months I never cared any more.

Some Fredonia newspapers finally caught up with me. They had been sent by Ben Hudson the Editor of the Fredonia Herald. In them I found Calvin Apollo's address and looked him up one day, as he was stationed not far from me. After the usual two weeks we loaded on a small ship and crossed over to England again. There was a Liberty ship being loaded up

At Dawn

going to the states that was named the Raven. After spending two more weeks in England we boarded the Queen Mary and in five days we were in the New York harbor. It was here I promised the Lady Liberty that, "If I ever see you again it will be from your backside." I had my second Thanksgiving dinner on the water. It was pork chops, mashed potatoes and gravy. The Queen Mary was so big we never got seasick. When we got off, the Red Cross gave everyone a pint of fresh milk to drink. I didn't know anything could taste so good. We had to drink powdered milk for twenty-two months and no ice cream because of undulant fever in the cattle over there. I had trouble realizing I was going home at last.

Here we were at Camp Shanks, New York again but no snow. We were fed a wonderful steak dinner with all the trimmings then went into a room one-on-one to listen to how we could enlist again and do anything we had already trained for. All I could remember was K rations, C rations or No rations at all so I never re-enlisted.

We were fed two meals per day while on a train or boat so I volunteered for K.P. on our way from New York to Camp Chaffee, Arkansas so I could get more to eat. It was slow going at Camp Chaffee. They were over crowded with so many coming home at one time. We were issued new uniforms there. That is the one I can still get into after so many years. Five of us from Kansas were discharged the same day. The M.P.s told us that at the edge of camp there would be people who would drive us to Wichita, Kansas for $45 or $50 each, but that some of them would suggest a certain beer joint on the way that was a good place to have fun. They would then slip knockout drops in your drink and you would wake up with no money and no car to take you to Wichita. The five of us took a bus for about $6 each.

We had a six hour layover in Oklahoma City to catch another bus so we all went to a restaurant and ordered whatever we craved to eat. I ordered one half of a peach pie with a pint of ice cream on it and a chocolate malt. Each one ordered something just as crazy. The waitress bent down and said, "The manager doesn't allow any drinking of alcohol in here." Our leader said, "Lady, there isn't a man here that has had a drink of alcohol for over eighteen months. We are just ordering what we crave the most." She got a big laugh out of that.

We spent some of our layover time in a place like the USO buildings we were used to. This one was run by a church. We made it into Wichita and all went our separate ways. I caught a bus to Toronto, Kansas then got a ride with a salesman on to Fredonia. I went to Babes Cafe and called Freda Maxwell to have Dad pick me up. That was the end of a long trail for me and I was tired and weary.

FINAL THOUGHTS

As we were going ashore in Normandy a recruit yelled, "You've heard about it and read about it but this is it!" There was simply no turning back.

I wouldn't take a million dollars for what I saw and did but I wouldn't want to do it again for ten million.

Alfred Beard
Photo taken in 1943 before going to war

On Guard Duty at Liege, Belgium.

German Pill Box for machine guns in the streets of Liege, Belgium.

June 1945 in one of the many narrow streets of Liege, Belgium.

German Robot Bomb crashing to earth in England.

Alfred Beard in 1945 after being wounded at Saint Lo, France.

Alfred and Obie Ligon on bombed out railroad bridge in Germany. Alfred on the right in both photos.

Ernest Pasada on the left who came to Alfred's aid when being threatened by the man on the right who had a dagger.

PART III
Family – Friends – Special Memories

CHAPTER 10

The first week I was home I went to the Fredonia Courthouse on business and when I entered the hallway I saw Billy Brown. Now Billy was the fourteenth man who joined our volunteer group. Someone who didn't know better put him in charge of the rest of us. Billy liked his alcohol and was pretty much wiped out by the time our bus reached Oscaloosa, Kansas. The rest of us had to have a signed pass before leaving the bus for lunch. He wouldn't cooperate and we tried everything we could think of but he wouldn't sign our passes. When we reached Leavenworth, Kansas Billy fell out of the bus and landed in a heap on the sidewalk. An officer came over and asked, "Who's in charge of this bunch?" We all pointed down to Billy and said, "He is."

We were separated and I never saw him after that. Now I was quite surprised to see him painting the walls in the Courthouse and remarked, "Why Billy, I didn't know you were a painter." "I am for 30 days" he said, never missing a stoke.

When spring came I was called to work at the Alfalfa Mill on April 4, 1946. Jack and Buss McGinnis worked at the mill the same time I did. We were sent to Coyville to cut alfalfa and stopped at the restaurant there for pie and coffee. We got Jack to laughin' about something and one of the five guys at the counter mimicked his laugh. Jack let it pass but when it happened the second time Jack was out of his chair challenging them all.

Buss started eating his pie as fast as he could and told me, "All we have to do is keep 'em off his back." Jack was an ex-Marine and wouldn't have needed much help. Now three of the five walked out the door and left. The other two sat at the counter quiet as you please.

As alfalfa was being cut I was loading it onto the truck by pitchfork. I had two-thirds of a load when I smelled a copperhead snake. They have a very distinct odor when mad or scared and since I didn't know which I was being very careful. It's been my experience that, if you wish to try it, you can stomp a copperhead and kill it, but by stomping a rattler's head you just make him mad and he can become very aggressive.

Suddenly I felt a sharp pain on my ankle. I thought I had received my first snakebite until I found I had been stung by a bumblebee.

I worked 12-hour shifts loading hay 7 days a week. That was a record for me and didn't leave much time for anything else.

At Dawn

A friend did, however, set me up on a blind date with a lovely young lady by the name of Sybil Manning. We liked each other right from the start. She also had the prettiest golden blond hair I ever saw.

When I found out she didn't know how to drive I decided to teach her. I had an old 1934 Ford Coup that was nothing to brag about so off to the pasture we went. I had her shift through all the gears over and over until she was getting good at it. I took her out on the road and we started off real nice until she saw a bad place in the roadway. She put her foot on the brake but hit the accelerator instead, got scared and turned toward the ditch. We took out three fence posts before I could turn off the key.

I backed the car out of the ditch and Sybil developed a bad headache from the scare so I took her home. I went back, fixed the fence posts and pounded the dents out of my fender. She never wanted to drive again.

I was working so many hours that one night I told her we should think about getting married so we could have more time together. She agreed and we were married on June 5, 1946. We managed to dodge the shivaree gang for a few days but at the picture show one night we came out to see too many cars parked close to mine. We walked to my sister's place and I drove her car while she and her husband got in ours. Sure enough, as they drove away a whole gang of cars backed out and took after them. We joined in the group chasing our own car. They finally got my car stopped so I walked up front and asked, "What's the hold up?" They grabbed me and put Sybil in a wheelbarrow and started around the square. I was crowding the inside curb but my brother-in-law crowded me to the outside. That took a lot more pushing. We made it around then went home for treats for everyone.

We then learned there was a city cop that lived in an apartment on the square who complained about the noise keeping him awake. Afterwards the city stopped all shivarees around the square.

One evening we were driving by the Police Station when Herb Hare and a big cop from Coyville came running out of the Station waving their guns so I screeched to a halt. They ran up to the car and said, "We want a cigar!"

On another evening we went out to my folks to visit. They went out to milk their cows and we were in the house by ourselves except for a big cat that was asleep back in a corner. We got to scuffling around and the cat got scared, climbed the curtain, broke the lamp chimney and knocked things all over the place before I could get him out the door. I was getting worried how much he was going to cost me. We did our scuffling outside after that.

When we were married about two years we bought a little house on 10th street in Fredonia. I was putting in a kitchen sink and had the window out. Sybil was standing in front of the window getting a glass of

Sharon Lambert

water and I stepped up from the outside and said, "BOO." She threw the glass of water right in my face. I guess I asked for that one.

I had left my hammer in the middle of the kitchen floor and she came along and stubbed her toe. She threw the hammer right through the screen door. I asked her later what happened and with a twinkle in her eye she said, "The cat did it." We did laugh and have a lot of fun no matter what happened in our lives.

Besides the big blue cat, we had a little Beagle dog. He had a bed in the back but liked to sleep on the divan. I walked past one night and he opened one eye and went back to sleep. Later Sybil got up. When he heard her he was off that couch and in his own bed in a flash.

We were beginning a wonderful marriage trip together. I was reminded of my prayer on the battlefield in Normandy. I prayed, "Lord please let me live through this even if I have to be wounded. I want to make it home and find a good wife." He answered everything I asked of Him.

When we married, all the money I had was my mustering out pay plus what I had saved from my back pay. We had enough to buy a car and some furniture and a down payment on a small tractor. By this time I was working at the Skelly Filling Station in Fredonia.

One day a hearse from Wichita pulled in on its way to Arkansas to pick up a body. The driver wanted me to check his transmission oil. I got in the hearse and pulled it up on the lift. There was a man asleep in the back who raised up and said, "Hey, let me out before you raise it up." I really think they did it on purpose to get a laugh out of me. They did.

A young man on a motorcycle drove by one afternoon and yelled, "I'm going around the block and into your grease rack so slam the door down behind me." There was a woman in a car trying to catch him. It seems she couldn't see well and was driving down the middle of the street when the young man passed her on the wrong side. It made her so mad she took after him and had been chasing him all over town.

While sweeping the inside driveway one day a dog trotted by that had slobbers all around his mouth. I stood real still and he never even looked at me. He crossed the street and got up on a dirt pile where work was being done on what is now Dennison Welding. The dog laid down in the shade of some weeds. Soon two Fredonia Police drove in and asked if I had seen a dog frothing at the mouth. I told them he was laying on that dirt pile looking at them. They jumped out of the car and shot him. I worked every other Sunday at the Station and one Sunday a man and his wife drove in and asked me to check his tires, radiator, water, wash his windshield and put in $1.00 worth of gas. He then proceeded to scold me for working on Sunday. I said, "Sir, I do not own this station. I just work here and as long as anyone comes in and demands service on Sunday it will be open." His wife started laughing and he drove away with a red face.

I worked there for eighteen months then got bold and tried farming. We had to live in old houses without electricity or indoor plumbing.

I was walking by the kitchen door one day just as my wife threw her pan of dishwater out the door right on my chest. It embarrassed her so much she always walked out and poured it in a ditch after that. I was rather pleased about that too. Soon we had running water to make life easier for her. The only things she didn't like about living in the country were the storms and the variety of snakes.

After a few years I asked Sybil if she wanted me to take her back to town and a better life. She said no, that she was happy just being with me. Praise God.

I worked a few years for the Maxwell Ranch and other farmers. We didn't have much but we were happy. We were also getting a family; soon our little daughter, Donna, was born. One afternoon I was loading some milo when I saw a blacksnake go into the truck. When I unloaded the grain the next day it wasn't in there. I crawled under the truck to grease the joints and there was the snake on the frame. Every time I tried to hit him with a board he pulled his head back. Sybil came walking by so I said, "Honey, would you wiggle this stick under here for me?" She got down and wiggled the stick and I got the snake. She said, "What am I doing this for?" I answered, "So I could get this blacksnake." She took off for the house. I was lucky to get anything to eat that day. By the time we were living on the Hudson Ranch we had a little boy named Thomas. There were a series of storms that came each night for a week or more and we would go to the cellar. This particular night Sybil said, "I'm going to put my clothes on the chair so I can get ready quick." An especially bad storm woke us during the night and she ran three trips around the bed before she could stop.

She took the baby and I carried our little girl. We were making a run for the cellar, which was about 30 yards away when she slipped on the porch and sat down, hard. I said, "Hold on, I'll be right back to get you." Before I reached the cellar she passed me and down into the cellar she and the baby went. She was so afraid of storms. In the following years, two more little sons joined the family. They are Delbert and Dwight.

One afternoon I was coming toward the house on my tractor and saw her throw her buckets of well water in the air and run for the house. I went in and asked her what was going on. She was barefooted and a snake, called a blue racer, got tangled up in her feet so away she went.

Sharon Lambert

Another time she saw a snake right by the house. She went out the back door, picked up a big rock, leaned out the window and smashed him with it. She was learning to take care of herself.

Our neighbors, the Jay Yoeman's, lived nearby and asked me to keep an eye on his place while they were on vacation. One moonlit night I walked around his buildings and house real slow and didn't find anything out of place. Sybil was sitting on our front porch, but when I walked back to the house she grabbed the kids and ran inside. I asked her why she did that and she said, "I just saw you walk by going west a little while ago." I got my rifle, let out a yell and put a few bullets through the treetops. We never found any more tracks in the dust after that. Fred Lambert was under sheriff at the time and told me they found some stolen guns in a house over the hill from me. The guy either left the country or was in jail for we never had any more trouble.

CHAPTER 11

I've always enjoyed fishing and setting limb lines. One summer I was on Frank Bakers river and parked my pick-up in some sandburs. It was dark when I finished. I got in my pick-up but it wouldn't move. I used my flashlight to check under the back axel and there was my very own jack holding it in the air. The next morning Frank came out to see what I had caught on my lines. He had an oh, so innocent look on his face. I talked a little while then I asked, "You wouldn't know why I got my knees in sandburs last night would you?" He just exploded in laughter. I've known of several people who've set lines on Frank that had the hook straightened. The limb was always partly broke so they put on a bigger hook on a bigger limb trying to catch that huge fish. Frank always carried pliers in his boat so figure that one out...

I also got into coyote hunting and really enjoyed it. Bill Ward had two real fast hounds and joined me on many a hunt. We turned loose around Pratt cabin one night, jumped a coyote and the race headed south. We drove toward the south road, stopped to listen and here came my old slow hound on a coyote trail of his own. Now Frank Baker was driving us in his jeep, and was never one to get excited over a coyote, so they put the windshield down and Bill loaded Frank's shotgun. I was in the back holding on for dear life. Frank drove Bill right up on the coyote real fast just before he got to the break of the hill. Then 'BOOM' down went the coyote but you don't stop a jeep right now. Before Frank stopped he ran over the dead coyote and went between several huge rocks before stopping. We picked up what was left of the coyote and my old slow dog then heard Bill's dogs with their own coyote under a cliff west of the pear orchard. Boy, what a ride.

The next time our hounds ran a coyote in the drain pipe of a pond. Frank got a piece of barbed wire about eight feet long, spread the ends apart a little and twisted it into the coyotes fur. He was pulling him out when he noticed his glove was also twisted into his end of the wire.

He hollered, "Alfred I need help I can't get loose." I grabbed a stick between my hands and held it out to an angry coyote who grabbed it in his mouth. I rolled him over and Frank jumped on him and tied his mouth shut. We put him in a gunnysack and went on hunting.

57

Sharon Lambert

My hunting buggy was an old Model A Ford with the top cut off. It had 16 inch wheels on the back and 19 inch wheels on the front. I always carried my rifle in a rack right beside me. One morning I walked up the hill at daylight, sat down looking east and went to sleep. I woke up looking a coyote in the face. I slowly raised my rifle, shot and watched a scared coyote run away. I went back to the house, put up a target, stepped off 100 yards and shot. I was shooting two feet to the side. Now sights do not move on their own. I remembered I had hauled two guys in the recent past. Frank Baker and Bill Ward. The sights could be turned with your fingers while going down the road but I never did get either one to admit doing it. That will just be an unsolved mystery.

We had a young fella come on one of our hunts down south of the Stryker Ranch. He had a new jeep but no experience. He wanted to ride with Frank and learn what a jeep would do—foolish guy.

Now there was a big hill with a ridge that came out to the south and just dropped almost straight down. It was so steep that grass wouldn't grow on it. This kid was riding in the back of Frank's jeep, which was running fast and over the ridge they went. That kid left the jeep in a flying leap. Frank got stopped at the bottom and said, "I thought you wanted to learn what a jeep would do." That was the last lesson he ever asked for.

If there was anything Frank was better at than fishing and hunting coyotes, it was country fire fighting. My sister, Margaret Ferguson, used to live north of Delaware Springs and fires were a very common thing every year up there. One fire was coming towards the Spring from the west before fire trucks could get there. I had a barrel of water, six buckets and sacks. I drove into the Spring and the old Gent was usually real cranky as to where you drove but when I told him what I had on my truck he said, "Park anywhere and never mind about the flowers." Sonny Worrell drove in behind me with enough high school boys to use all my buckets and sacks. We kept the fire from doing any damage at the Spring. The old Gent sent me tomato plants for several years after that.

Another time I was up there with just one bucket and sack. The fire was all over the timber. Along came Frank with his fire truck but no crew. He put me to driving and he ran the hose. We put out the northwest fire when Frank asked, "Can we get through to the highway south of here?" I told him, "There is a road but it has trees growing in it up to four inches through." He said, "Put the truck in low gear and hit all your trees with the left side of your bumper." We were soon out on the highway and heading east. The sheriff was there to slow down traffic and another fire truck showed up to help. We went into the Spring's buildings to wet down the roofs. We were doing a good job when we heard a lot of yellin'. There was

58

a guy on the other side of the roof and Frank was soaking him. We ran out of water so I backed up to a small fishpond. We pumped it almost dry then had to put out a fire coming in from the south. Glen Duckworth and his wife came driving up with a big chocolate cake. It lasted about as long as a handful of snow on a hot stove but it was sure good.

The train used to throw out a lot of sparks going up the grade just south of me and set fires along the right-of-way in dry weather. Frank came and was fighting fire up a pretty good gully on Maxwell's. A bystander said, "He'll have to come back out and go around the other side to get in." I said, "You don't know Frank Baker do you? All he needs is for us to follow up with a bucket and wet sack to put out anything that might start up again." That fire was out in no time and Frank was ready for more.

I finally got on at the Cement Plant with the help of Faye Ward and Clifford Timmons. I was so grateful for their help. I received as much for 40 hours as I did for 56 hours at a previous job.

One of my jobs at the plant was at the rock crusher. We had to keep the rock flowing down onto a belt that would carry it to the grinding mills. Once a young man was in the rock bin and rock slid down around his legs trapping him. There had been a man killed that way years before. I braced my feet on either side of him and said, "Now I can't pull you out but I can hold you until the rock feeds out." How glad I was that the day turned out good for both of us.

The plant had breakdowns and messes to clean up if you were willing to work all kinds of overtime. I worked all I could stand and put it into a savings account.

The years just seemed to fly by and the children were grown. I retired at age 63 and had enough money to buy my pretty little wife a new prefab home and a new pickup with a camper for us to travel in. Was she ever happy. Then one night my chest and left arm hurt all night. I went to the Doctor the next day and was put in the hospital in Intensive Care without visitors for about five days. I had plenty of time for some serious thinking. When I got home I went to church with Sybil and we accepted Jesus into our hearts, which was what she wanted all along.

For the next fourteen years we had fun going to Montana hunting sapphires, to Colorado panning for gold and Arkansas to the diamond mine. We never found any diamonds but the hunt was worth it.

Rainbow Valley has always had a lot of wildlife because it's a little more secluded than some areas. A few years back I heard tales of cougar sightings. The first one I saw was in an 80 acre area not far from my home. I was looking around at the top of the hill and looked to my left just as a big cat was crouched down, belly rubbing the ground, sneaking away.

Sharon Lambert

I told Bill Ward and he asked me what I had to drink that day. Later we were driving south of my place near the railroad track when Bill started hollering, "Look there!" I put the brakes on and looked for a train but it was one of the big cats crossing the road. Seems Bill took a sip out of the same bottle. I've seen another one crouching in a road ditch nearby that was darker brown in color.

My most interesting experience came one hunting season when I was coming home from the pasture carrying a big turkey. It was late and I had about a mile and a quarter to walk through thick timber. I was almost home when I heard a cougar close by growling, or caterwauling I call it. Had I known he was out in that timber behind me he would have had a very easy turkey dinner.

CHAPTER 12

There are often unexpected challenges in life and we've had some too. During hunting season my son shot a deer and I knew he hit it hard so I went in the timber and found it. As I was pulling it out to a clearing I had some awful chest pains. I sat down and my chest quit hurting after awhile. The Doctor sent me to the heart hospital where I had three bypasses. I've not had any trouble since. Then in 2000 my wife developed Alzheimer's, which is a difficult thing, but we managed. I kept her with me until the end, which came in April of 2007, after 60 years and 10 months of marriage. I'm so thankful for all those wonderful years we had together, the fun vacations we took. I miss my dear wife but have the comfort of knowing she's in Heaven and I'll see her there some day. Just think of it; no more sickness, no more pain or sorrow. Thank you so much Lord.

The other day God asked me, in His plan, to witness to an old friend. I was so happy He chose me. Just maybe God can use me again. I tell Him, "Here I am, use me wherever you need me."

I move at a slower pace now. No need to hurry as much. I get to all the places I want to anyhow. I keep busy visiting friends and neighbors and attending Bible class and Church; volunteering for Memorial Day and Veterans Day parades. I still fit into my Army uniform. I wear it proudly.

I enjoy my weekly volunteer duty on the church bus route herding a load of kids to Royal Rangers and Missionette's, both youth activities at my church, The First Assembly in Fredonia. The kids call me 'The old man on the bus.' Some days it's similar to my military guard duty but that's O.K. Kind of reminds me of some kids I knew in Rainbow Valley a long time ago.

The Senior Citizen Center is a favorite place to visit with friends and the monthly hot biscuit and gravy breakfast gathers in more of my favorite crowd.

I'm presently teaching my son and grandson my hunting and trapping tricks that I've learned throughout my lifetime. You've got to know the critter's habits then go about out-smarting him. When I'm finished I will just loaf and visit. I can't figure how time went by so fast but it's all gone somewhere. I have my children and grandchildren, extended family, a host of the greatest friends anywhere and wonderful memories of them all.

The End

1946 Wedding Photo.
Sybil & Alfred Beard

Sybil Beard in the 1950's.

EPILOGUE

This book endeavors to present to you the true story Alfred Beard relayed to me in the spring and summer of 2008.

I was inspired by the humorous events Alfred chose to focus on. These stories lift us from the recounts of war. It's the measure of a man. One who's put the past where it belongs and who looks to the future with courage.

Sharon Lambert

Printed in the United States
206271BV00002B/325-438/P